COLUMBUS AND BEYOND
Views from Native Americans

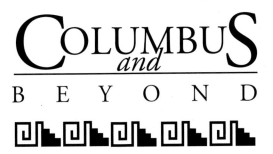

COLUMBUS and BEYOND

Views from Native Americans

PAULA GUNN ALLEN
and
LEE FRANCIS III

•

LINDA HOGAN

•

SIMON ORTIZ

•

CARTER REVARD

•

RAY A. YOUNG BEAR

ISBN 1-877856-06-01

Library of Congress Number 91-067396

©1992, Southwest Parks and Monuments Association, Tucson, Arizona

Edited by Randolph Jorgen

Production Supervision by Ron Foreman

Design by Kimura/Bingham Design, Tucson, Arizona

Printed on recycled paper by Arizona Lithographers, Tucson, Arizona

Cover Painting:
"Admiral of the Ocean Sea,"
by N. Scott Momaday
Courtesy of LewAllen Gallery, Santa Fe, New Mexico
Photo by Dan Morse

CONTENTS

INTRODUCTION

Five hundred years ago Columbus and his cohorts arrived in America as the first in an inexorable tide of Europeans to follow. They began a worldwide process of ecological, cultural, spiritual, and economic change unparalleled in human history, a process that intensifies to this day. The following essays were written on the occasion of this anniversary. In the United States and Europe, at least, 1992 has mostly been taken as cause for celebration, and even (predictably) as an opportunity for commercial exploitation. After all, it marks a half a millenium of "success," the transmission of European culture into a vast and "virgin" land; the flowering of that culture into new forms directed by higher ideals; and the development of the greatest treasure trove of natural resources known into the most productive and powerful nation on earth. But some people are not celebrating, and in fact are quite sober at this juncture. Why?

It is not surprising that loudest among the voices of protest are many Native Americans, including the six who contributed the following essays. They are part of a growing reevaluation our history, of Columbus himself—dethroning an American folk hero, the myth of the man, his mission, and his accomplishments—and of the much greater issue of the entire five hundred years of European presence in the Americas. They point out the fact of the obliteration of millions of native people, and of hundreds of distinct cultures. They recite the legacy of physical and economic enslavement. They point to the hypocrisy of a society that professes to have been created to ensure justice for all and rights for minorities, but was founded by denying those rights to its original inhabitants and expropriating their land—their very identity and basis for life. They ask, where is the appreciation for the knowledge and wisdom of Indian cultures commensurate with what those cultures have to offer? Where is the treatment of the land based on respect and on the knowledge of how to sustain life for millennia, not just until the next tax return or election year? Where are the legal, social, and economic policies that acknowledge Native Americans and the ways of native cultures as equal partners in the life of the hemisphere?

Some have viewed the opening of the Americas as the *tabula rasa* European society had unconsciously been yearning for, the chance to start fresh and show how good it truly could become, if only that tired old continent could be left behind. The Americas were indeed an opportunity, but they were not an empty slate, for they were not uninhabited. It was indicative of the personal and cultural immaturity of the Europeans that they took the natives primarily as obstacles in their myopic path, and certainly not as equals to learn from and work with. A recurrent theme of the essayists in this volume is a sadness for opportunities lost—a personal sadness for the loss of their cultures and people, and a broader sadness for opportunities lost to entire nations in that failed chance for partnership. There is a sense that much could have been gained for both natives and foreigners had there been less arrogance and greed, and more respect and cooperation. But even more important is to claim lost opportunities that can still be regained, those that still await our diligent efforts toward a better world and a more just society.

There is much wisdom nonnatives can learn today from Native Americans past and present, and much we can do to right past and present wrongs. Every culture holds a unique fund of knowledge and embodies its own set of values. These attributes create in each culture its own particular strengths in knowing how to live well, strengths which others are, at a minimum, impoverished by rejecting out of hand or from shallow understanding.

Our past is multicultural, and so too shall be our future. Will we choose to accept the gifts of cultures other than our own—which can only be done through humility and respect—or will we continue to reject them as inferior, as the vanquished? How vulnerable will we be to a reconsideration of our history and of our society? We must not, out of discomfort, seek to avoid the complexity of our past, nor of the present unresolved moral and practical questions raised by it.

America's national parks are focal points for the interpretation of our history. Southwest Parks and Monuments Association (SPMA) aids the interpretive efforts of the National Park Service through sales and publication of educational materials. The following five essays are presented by SPMA as part of its commitment to make that interpretive presentation as complete and balanced as possible.

The essayists are among the foremost Native American writers today, invited by virtue of their ability to discern and express the pulse of their own peoples, although they would in no way claim to be official representatives.

The purpose of poets and writers is to check our headlong lurch into the future, to give us pause to question the wisdom of our ways. These six were charged with addressing not only the historical context of Europeans occupying America, but also the awkward practical question of how shall people of conscience, knowing our history, live today? Each has approached it from a different angle, and most with a gentleness and obliqueness typically Native American. You may have to read between the lines to extrapolate your own direction. But here are the views of six in earnest offering.

—Randolph Jorgen,
June 1992,
Tucson, Arizona

LINDA HOGAN

Linda Hogan, Chickasaw Native American, was born in 1947 in Denver and grew up in Oklahoma. A poet and teacher, she is the author of *Calling Myself Home, Daughters, I Love You,* and *Eclipse.* Her works also have been published in the anthologies *Earth Power Coming, The Remembered Earth,* and *Survival This Way,* as well as *The Beloit Poetry Journal, Hiram Review, The Little Magazine, Greenfield Review,* and *Prairie Schooner.* She lives in Idledale, Colorado.

Journeys
and Other Stories

by Linda Hogan

It is daybreak in the canyon. A horned owl has just become silent. The seepage on canyon walls is in the thin shape of ancient people stepping out from stone as if to witness morning. Clay. Stone. Sand. In the first light of the southwestern land, there is a hint of moisture. Soon there are shadows, then lizard tracks crossing sand, the curling motion of a snake moving into warm sun. These are a language land speaks to travelers in canyons. It is the whisper that draws us to land, a language something like a memory inside us, of wilderness, of an ancient past. It has a beautiful and magnetic longing to it, this mystery of hands on canyon walls, the stories of people who built dwellings of stone so well the walls remain long after the people are gone.

Most of us journey to the land because of that mystery. It is a pilgrimage of sorts. We need, without the saying of it, to see the arrow-shaped deer tracks, fossils, shards of an older civilization, to read the language of an ancient past that is still being spoken in stone, by wind, in petroglyphs. We want to weave together the threads of where we come from with what we are now and where we are going. Our human journey here joins with the stories of snake, owl, lizard, the far-traveling winds and curving waters. We gauge our place by these stories, by our movement, and by our defining the fierce human struggle for survival, for whatever meaning and revelation live in this burning light of day.

We bring to this terrain not only our individual stories, but the larger one that contains them, the one we call history—EuroAmerican history, that is, which has become the main surviving record of what has taken place on this continent.

Most of us think of this history as the accurate record of what has been before us, but we seldom consider how it has been logged and told. Less often do we consider what material is added or removed in the telling, but time after time, new information, new stories, rise up through the words and pages of history to assert themselves and shift the story all about. And accounts of the conquest of the American continent are some of the stories still being revised and retold as many contemporary historians are searching not for a story of European arrival on this continent, but for the story of what actually took place.

In considering the new information, it might be best for us to think of those fifteenth-century voyages in their context of time and place, especially since we are finding that we have reached the limits of a way of thinking and living that had its origins in that world where the thinkers and scientists held that the earth was flat and that there was grave danger in traveling toward the ends of water or land. A man, a ship, they feared, might be carried down into the land of demons, the dangerous, animal-filled wilderness, and fiery hell.

At that time, what is now called "America" was not yet even a seed planted in the mind of its explorers and conquerors; there were no prophecies about this continent; no land mass was even accounted for at that time. A heaven with gold-paved streets lived in the minds of Europeans. Their God didn't live on land but in a distant place with mansions, gold, and winged people, those who had lived well enough to escape the earth. The dominant belief system looked away from land. It was not based, as tribal systems are, on matter, earth, or even the sanctity of life. It did not value the plants or animals that fed the people. The living world was not a sacred, alive thing. The people did not learn to know their own land. They did not know how to maintain a working agriculture that was successful without depleting the soil, and by the time three ships set sail in search of what they came to call "Paradise," the European continent was deforested, the land exhausted. Theirs was a failed belief system even in their own words and biblical terms; "by their fruits shall you know them," because the fruits of that society were hunger, plague, and violence. The system, in that time, did not deliver the Europeans. There was no salvation in it. Not only was it lacking in depth and compassion, but it hadn't established significant values or paid heed to the most plain and common sense that would allow the land to thrive.

In his book *The Conquest of Paradise*, Kirkpatrick Sale writes about European life in the fifteenth century, that "death was so daily, brutality so commonplace, destruction of the animate and inanimate so customary that it is shocking even in our own age of mass destruction."

Out of this wounded, destroyed world, men set sail in search of resources they could take home with them. These were voyages of desperation and necessity. And as much as they did not know or understand the land they were leaving, the one already laid waste, they did not have the capacity to understand, learn, or even describe the ancient and viable world they came, without clear vision, to call "new."

As their own stories note, they wanted what humans could never have—cities of gold, the elixir of youth, eternal life. And just as they were lost in these childlike desires, they were lost physically at sea.

They sailed into a deep fatigue. It was a bitter journey as they searched for land. In the words of Columbus, from his journals, everything became a sign of land: birds that were believed not to live out at sea, rafts of floating vegetation. On September 19, 1492, rain fell and "this was certain indication of land." On the 21st, he reports that his men saw a whale, "which is sign that they were near land." On September 26, what they thought was land revealed itself as only a cloud. The sailors were "alarmed and depressed." On October 6, they saw "certain land," but, proceeding in that direction, they found only fresh vegetation and what they thought were land birds. The day of October 10 the men "complained of the long voyage."

Finally, on the October 11 they saw a stick carved by a human hand floating on the sea and knew they were near land. On landing, they were greeted by people, described by Columbus in a letter to the king. He wrote that "they have no iron or steel or weapons, nor are they fitted to use them …because they are marvellously timorous. They have no other arms than spears made of canes." He also noted their generosity, that "they refuse nothing that they possess, if it be asked of them; on the contrary, they invite any one to share it and display as much love as if they would give their hearts." These are the same traits that Columbus later said would make the people good "slaves" in the service of the king. That first encounter with the Arawaks proved to be a fatal one that would lead to the extinction of the entire indigenous population.

The old land, new to the voyagers, bore bountiful fruit, and was green and rich. But it was seen as having no importance because it did not, at first, yield the mythical riches and gold that the Europeans sought and valued. From a contemporary perspective these men's ignorance about the world was a not-knowing that had devastating consequences for people and for the land, as much as it had in their own land, with their own people. Their system of belief, their manner of living, came full force into collision with other systems, ones that had been tried and time-tested and whose key common element was a balanced and healthy relationship with land, wilderness, and other forms of life.

The Indian people had, and in many places still have, considerable knowledge of the land. Survival depended on it, as it does now. Before the Europeans arrived, Peacemaker of the Iroquois Nation had spoken his own vision of a healthy society where human beings whose minds are healthy desire peace. Righteousness, Peacemaker said, occurs when people put their minds and emotions in harmony with the flow of the universe:

The principles of Righteousness demand that all thoughts of prejudice, privilege or superiority be swept away and that recognition be given to the reality that the creation is intended for the benefit of all equally— even the birds and animals, the trees and the insects, as well as the humans."

Centuries of this understanding and working relationship between people and the rest of the natural world went unrecognized by the new arrivals. The life of this American continent, the vision of a balanced system, did not fit into the European world view and categories of thought. What was old, what was time-tested and functional, was changed, broken, and bent to fit the very system that had made the voyages necessary. Natural systems, now called ecology, were simply not understood by those who came from the European cultures and belief systems.

It has become increasingly clear to many historians and thinkers that the conquerors were mentally unbalanced, even delusional men. They were on an impossible journey, fueled by insatiable wants. It could be said that this obsessive search became the center of a madness, one with severe biological and ecological consequences, a madness that destroyed volumes of highly evolved medical information, astronomy and mathematics as it burned the words and memories of those the Europeans believed to be savages. This madness became our joint legacy, of Indians and non-Indians alike, a shared heritage that still defines our lives, is still lived out in the daily ongoing violation of land, human, and animal life. The attempt to shape the world according to what had not worked in Europe did not work here either.

We are at the end of that way of knowing, that madness. It is as if we have finally reached the limit of that once-flat world, and are falling over. We are almost at the end of ocean, wilderness, and fragile desert. The world is finite, and only now is the intelligence of the natural world, long understood by Native Americans, revealing itself to science as researchers discover that birds find their way to an unknown home by magnetic fields and the sounds of fish beneath the water, that the songs of whales are not only complex and intelligent, but that these songs are able to stun squid into stillness. There is even now a newly emerging biology, one not based on the Darwinian model of survival of the fittest and evolution of individual organisms or species, but a biology that recognizes cooperation and relationship, one that allows for the health and survival of all, another concept that tribal people knew at the time of first white contact.

We stand together at the place where the failed European system of belief has led us, at the threshold to the endangered world, at limits stretched to breaking. Too much is moving over the edge, species and lives falling over the end of earth. We face the possibility of a lifeless earth, a future that will not house us. We have no choice but to face ourselves, history, our fears, and the challenge of change. This time there is no slipping over the horizon to find, magically, that the world will extend itself for us, beyond the horizon, beyond water or land.

If we are going to heal, we have to swallow the bitter tea of memory, to let our stories be re-membered. And it is not just us, nor the rest of the natural world that needs healing, but meaning, history, and destiny. We need to find a way to mend the wounds of a destructive past.

In whatever way we have come to this land, as tourists, residents, or pilgrims, we have come to find what is still unexplored and mysterious, within and without ourselves. We have come for the silence that embraces us, the feel of what's ancient, the safe fold in the universe that feeds our lives.

We are looking for a deepening, expanded, and liberating vision of the world, a different story to live by as we seek to restore the relationships between ourselves and land, between ourselves and others, between then and now.

We have traveled the distance of earth, the depths of water, traveled to the moon, explored the frozen blue-white poles of the planet, journeyed inside the ice and fire of earth, and what we know is that this is home, and that it demands understanding. Until we learn the land, we will not know who we are, it will turn against us, we will remain ignorant and small and helpless.

Hungry for the dimensions of our lives, we think we are not snake, fish, bird, but there is an uncanny knowing that we are part of sand, wind, water, fire, the elemental world millions of years old. We are carbon, hydrogen, oxygen. We are song and possibility, part of *the* story, moment by moment holding history in a hand as it unfolds. The land is our elder. It knows and speaks an older history. It has a living memory, a terrestrial intelligence we have betrayed. It holds its own stories and is alive.

It could have been another way, the coming together of all these stories. Think of what it could have been. Think of what it yet may be.

SOURCES:
Peacemaker's speech appears in *A Basic Call to Consciousness*, Akwesasne Notes Press, Mohawk Nation via Rooseveltown, NY. Excerpts of journals are from *The Diary of Christopher Columbus*. Other information is in Kirkpatrick Sale's book *The Conquest of Paradise*.

Simon J. Ortiz

Simon J. Ortiz, born in 1941, is from
Acoma Pueblo, New Mexico. A former tribal
official and college instructor of Native
American literature and creative writing, he is
presently writing full time. Although well
known as a poet, he is writing fiction again as
well as working on television and film projects.
His publications include *Going for the Rain, A
Good Journey, Fightin': New & Collected Stories,
From Sand Creek,* and others, and the
forthcoming *Woven Stone* and *After and
Before the Lightning.*

Coming Into Being: 500 Years Later

by Simon J. Ortiz

Initial Encounter

At Acoma Pueblo in New Mexico, an announcement is made from time to time: *Yaaka Hanoh naitrah guh.* It is about a Corn (Maize) Dance ceremony upcoming in the pueblo. But the figurative meaning of the statement also must be taken into account, because *Yaaka Hanoh naitrah guh* aptly translates to "the Corn people will come about," or "will happen." Through the ceremonial ritual dancing and singing, the Corn People indeed will come into existence. During the time of the Corn Dance the corn will symbolically be a part of the daily life of Acoma Pueblo. The significance of this is realized not only during the ceremony, however; people with this awareness know the sacred nature of maize and all life all of the time.

I wonder what Christopher Columbus and his men thought in A.D. 1492 when they first encountered Native American ritual ceremony. Through it did they find within themselves a meditative place? To indigenous people of the Western Hemisphere, who later came to be known as "Indians" and then as Native Americans, ritual ceremony is the act and experience of coming into being. With ceremony that includes prayer, meditation, song, and dance, Native Americans experience coming into spiritual consciousness in their own unique way. Perhaps this different understanding of spirituality helps explain the reaction by early Europeans to Native American people. They regarded them as superstitious, primitive, and childlike. Because of this misperception, other Europeans acquired only a limited view of Native Americans, one that to a large degree persists today. At the same time, Native Americans saw people of European background as demanding, rigid, judgmental, and exploitive. Since the "discovery," many changes have been wrought on Native American lives and culture by European people. To a much lesser extent have changes been effected by Native Americans on Europeans.

Columbus's discovery of the Western Hemisphere, an event of vast importance, was unexpected. At the same time, there likely were some Native Americans who saw "discovery" as destiny. Following Columbus's encounter with the Arawaks of the Bahamas, a partnership could have been initiated that would have benefited Europeans and Native Americans alike. But Columbus and his men were looking obsessively for gold, spices, and slaves. Though the Arawaks were generous toward Columbus and his men, they were also seen as people who could be taken advantage of, for Columbus primarily intended to enrich himself and to bring acclaim to his person. Thus the native people of the Americas were regarded with little or no respect by Europeans.

As archeological and anthropological evidence supports, tribal cultures and communities have existed in the Americas for somewhere between twelve and thirty thousand years. Within the mythic knowledge of Native American life are many references to prehistoric change. In a natural, organic world change is always occurring, and Native American people have never absolutely resisted or run away from change. Instead they have tried to creatively adapt to the demands of changes, whether these were earthquakes, droughts, or altered human social dynamics. Throughout the countless generations of Native American life before the arrival of European people and culture, life was considered an experience that people should learn from. It is unfortunate that the Europeans were not as open-minded about experience and knowledge; instead they insisted on their self-centered world vision, and as a result, often acted against their own interest. Had the Europeans been diplomatically sophisticated and mature, doubtless a strong, stable foundation for a beneficial society would have been established in the Americas.

Let's ponder the impact of "discovery" by Columbus and his men. Let's look at this as we keep in mind the Columbus quincentenary of 1992. Let's also consider the consequences relating to European decisions and actions.

After thirty-three days at sea in three ships, the Santa Maria, Niña, and the Pinta, land was sighted by a sailor named Rodrigo on October 12, 1492. The first man to sight land was supposed to get a yearly pension of ten thousand maravedis, but that wasn't the way it turned out for Rodrigo. Instead, Columbus claimed the prize for himself, saying he had seen a light the night before. Approaching an island in the Bahamas in the Caribbean Sea, Columbus, an Italian admiral, and his Spanish men were met by Arawaks, who swam out to meet them. The Arawaks lived in village communities and had a thriving agricultural livelihood, with principal crops of maize, yams, and cassavas. They were also craftspeople who could spin and weave, and they made tiny gold ornaments which they wore in their ears. When Columbus saw these ornaments, he immediately ordered that some Arawaks be held captive to get them to reveal the whereabouts of the gold ore.

Captives were also taken for slavery. In fact, before Columbus sailed from Spain, he promised the Spanish royalty he would bring them as much gold as they needed and as many slaves as they asked for on his voyage. Gold and slaves were the powerful impetus behind the European conquest of the Americas. Because of Columbus's extravagant report to the court of Spain, his second expedition was given seventeen ships and more than twelve hundred men. The expeditionary aim was clear: slaves and gold. Columbus and the Spaniards went from island to island in the Caribbean taking Native Americans as prisoners. Soon word spread about the intentions of the Europeans, and they found more and more empty villages. Nevertheless, in 1495, the Spaniards captured fifteen hundred Arawak men, women, and children and put them in pens. Subsequently, five hundred of the best Arawaks were chosen to be loaded onto ships bound for Spain. Two hundred died en route, and the rest were sold in Spain.

The Arawaks tried to resist, but they faced Spanish armor, muskets, swords, and horses. The Spanish hung them, burned many to death, and others began to commit suicide. Arawak infants were killed to save them from the Spaniards. In a couple of years, half of the two hundred and fifty thousand Arawaks of Haiti were dead, and by 1515 fifty thousand were left. By 1550 only five hundred survived and by 1650 none of the original Arawaks or their descendants were left on the island. This pattern of conquest—subjugation and genocide—was to be repeated countless times by Europeans and their descendants, from the shores of South America to the interior of North America. Almost no native community was immune from devastation caused by Europeans and their mad "progress."

In 1519, a Spanish armada led by Hernando Cortés landed at Vera Cruz. Funded by merchants and landowners, the expedition had one goal: to find gold. Moctezuma, the chief of the Aztecs, sent a hundred runners to Cortés with gold and silver presents, at the same time asking him to go away. Instead, Cortés began a death march from Aztec town to Aztec town. His strategy was simply to paralyze the will of the indigenous people by a sudden, fear-instilling deed. In Cholula, Cortés invited the leaders of the Cholula Nation to the town plaza, and when they came, the small Spanish army, mounted on horses, murdered the natives with cannon fire and crossbows. After looting the city of Cholula, they moved on to Mexico City. When the journey of death was over, Moctezuma was dead and Mexico City was shattered and under the absolute rule of the Spanish.

It was the same story in Peru, where Pizarro, another Spanish conquistador, also went for "the primitive accumulation of capital" (as later phrased by Karl Marx), seeking gold, slaves, and products of the soil. In the English colonial settlement areas of North America, the pattern of genocide and land theft was the same. By 1622, as the numbers of English settlements kept growing, the native population decided to put a stop to settlement. They attacked the colonists and killed 347 men, women, and children. Fourteen years later, in 1636, Puritans led by Captain John Mason killed about six hundred Pequots on the Mystic River near Long Island Sound. According to Dr. Francis Jennings, the Pequots learned three lessons from the Pequot War: (1) that the Englishmen's most solemn pledge would be broken whenever advantage conflicted with obligation; (2) that the English style of war had no limit or scruple or mercy; and (3) that weapons of Indian making were almost useless against weapons of European manufacture. The bottom line of these lessons was that the Native American population, estimated between 55 and 100 million at the eve of the "discovery" of the Western Hemisphere, was reduced drastically. Today the native population in North America is only around 2.5 million.

The other principal cause of Native American genocide was disease, especially smallpox, which raged in devastating epidemics through tribal populations. A Dutch traveler in New Netherlands in 1656 wrote of the natives there that "before the arrival of the Christians, and before the smallpox broke out amongst them, they were ten times as numerous as they are now, and that their population had been melted down by the disease, whereas nine-tenths of them have died."

Ultimately, the European invasion of the North and South American continents, utilizing massacres, deception, barbarism, and terror, was motivated by their desire for land and natural resources to be held as private property, which was the basis of Western civilization. But property and resources were owned in common by Native Americans. There were countless instances of Native American generosity and sharing when Europeans first came among them. For instance, in 1540 Francisco Vásquez de Coronado was welcomed and feted by the Pueblo people of the Rio Grande region in present-day New Mexico, even after he and his men had attacked the Pueblos at Hawikuh. He and his men were provided food, hides, and other supplies.

By 1598, Spanish rule in New Mexico was administered by soldiers and friars who were Iberian conquistadors born in Mexico. Colonization was aimed at enriching the Spanish church and state and satisfying personal ambitions. In December of that year, Acoma Pueblo was burned and razed by soldiers under Juan de Oñate, the first colonizer of present-day New Mexico. Clearly this was done to demonstrate to the other Pueblos the terrifying methods of conquest and control in the hands of the conquistadors. Subsequently, the sixteenth- and seventeenth-century Spanish colony was a parasite economically; it drew its living from Pueblo labor and captive slaves. The Spanish *encomendero* was a lord over Pueblo people, while the priests fought for control of Pueblo souls, labor, and resources.

The eighty-year colonial occupation of the Southwest, from 1598 to the Pueblo Revolt of 1680 and chiefly in the Rio Abajo and Rio Arriba regions of New Mexico, resulted in confusion and the destruction of Pueblo agriculture and society. *Estancias* were established which encroached on Pueblo lands, and many Pueblos went to live among the Apaches and Navajos. Pueblo communities were reduced from ninety-two in 1540 to a mere nineteen by the twentieth century.

The year 1680 saw the revolt by the Pueblos against Spanish oppression. At least twenty years of organized resistance produced a unified offensive by the Rio Grande Pueblos as well as the Zunis, Hopis, Utes, Apaches, and Navajos. Many lower class people, mulattos, mestizos, and Native American servants and slaves also revolted. The Spanish oppressors were driven southward at least as far as El Paso, from where they did not return for twelve years. When the Spanish returned to New Mexico in 1692, their relationship with the natives was in some instances improved. For example, land tenure of Pueblo people was spelled out to prevent Spanish settlement on Pueblo land. Also, destructive livestock, mainly cattle and sheep, were regulated by the crown for the protection of Pueblo agriculture, and in several instances, Spanish civil provisions stipulated that Pueblo villages receive land grants to increase their agricultural landholdings. Nevertheless, Spanish rule of the Pueblos, Navajos, Apaches, and other natives of the Southwest continued to be oppressive for the most part. There was intense competition between Spanish friars and colonial officials for Pueblo labor. Even after the Pueblo Revolt, Pueblo people were forced to work in sweat shops for long hours, producing commodities for Spanish officials.

SIGNIFICANCE OF CHANGE

In the latter decades of the fifteenth century, European civilization was convinced of its superiority, with Christianity and the "primitive accumulation of capital" largely behind this assurance. Its leaders, particularly those of England and Spain, had no doubts about the validity of their efforts; they were willing to risk whatever was required to gain wealth, power, and land. This mindset would become the political, economic, and civil policy of American Manifest Destiny later on, and American political leaders egotistically did not question their victimization of Native Americans.

The traditional livelihood of Native Americans before the arrival of Columbus was totally interdependent with the natural environment. Bartolome de las Casas, a Spanish priest, transcribed Columbus's journals and wrote a *History of the Indies*. His chronicles are the most thorough of any early European observer, describing the native lifestyle by such statements as, "They lack all manner of commerce, neither buying nor selling, and relying exclusively on their natural environment for maintenance. They are extremely generous with their possessions and by the same token covet the possessions of their friends and expect the same degree of liberality." But in book two of the *History*, de las Casas provides an account of the exemplary violence of the Spaniards led by Columbus, writing, "Our work was to exasperate, ravage, kill, mangle, and destroy; small wonder then, if they tried to kill one of us now and then. The Admiral [Columbus] it is true was blind as those who came after him, and he was so anxious to please the King that he committed irreparable crimes against the Indians."

The brutal policies and actions of the Spanish, and later the English, Portugese, Dutch, and French in North America, including genocide and land theft, have had disastrous effects upon Native Americans. Denying the savage tactics employed by Columbus and his men, and for the most part emphasizing only their so-called heroic exploits, is a political and ideological choice. This denial has been a major part of the justification for European and American land and natural resource grabs, particularly the land cession from Mexico per the Treaty de Guadalupe Hidalgo in 1848. In recent decades this has also determined the political and economic tactics toward Vietnam, Nicaragua, Chile, and Grenada.

The imposition of European lifestyles and, later, U.S. government policies upon Native Americans have drastically diminished their land base, curtailed self-government, forced a change from self-sufficiency to dependence on wage income, and brought about extensive socio-ideological changes. For example, selection of leaders has changed from reliance on traditional ideals and methods usually based on religious philosophy to popular elections. Nevertheless, Native Americans of the Southwest, especially the present-day nineteen Pueblos, insist on their own unique sociocultural system, with their own languages, government, landholdings, water and other natural resource rights, religion, and livelihood. They are convinced that their resistance against the powerful European and American forces facing them is to their benefit.

In recent decades, especially since the 1940s, the constant immigration of people to the U.S. of mixed ancestry (mestizos) from Latin America has resulted in an awareness of common interest and purpose between Latin Americans of mixed ancestry and Native Americans of North America. This is especially true of native people whose homeland is the southwestern U.S. Christopher Columbus and later European adventurers inspired defensive measures by Native Americans. In almost no instance have Native Americans been indifferent to Western capitalist and imperialist politics. The approaching decades will more than ever powerfully impact Native American people, who will continue to insist on their own native ways and rights. If finally the "discovery" of the Americas by Christopher Columbus means anything positive and creative it will be the recognition of and respect for Native American people by Anglo-Europeans and Americans.

Felix Cohen, a noted scholar of Native American law and philosophy, made the following observation in the 1940s: "Like the miner's canary, the Indian marks the shifts from fresh air to poison gas in our political atmosphere, and our treatment of Indians, even more than our treatment of other minorities, reflects the rise and fall in our democratic faith."

If only Admiral Columbus and those who followed would have had the sense of this, we would today have a much more positive social, economic, and political system for all.

CARTER REVARD

Osage Native American writer and teacher Carter Revard, born 1931 in Pawhuska, Oklahoma, is a Rhodes scholar who has taught at Amherst College and is now Professor of English at Washington University in St. Louis, Missouri. His works include *Cowboys and Indians, An Eagle Nation* to be published by the University of Arizona Press, and *Ponca War Dancers*. His poetry has been published in *River Styx, Sun Tracks, Voices of the Rainbow, The Remembered Earth*, and *Survival This Way*.

How Columbus Fell From the Sky and Lighted Up Two Continents

Columbus, Milton, Shakespeare, and the Osage and Navajo Creation Stories

by Carter Revard

Sublime achievement against great odds, sordid crimes against humanity: reading the logbooks and letters of Christopher Columbus, we meet both these facts. Columbus boldly went where no European before him had gone, and he led a small band of often-frightened and discouraged men with daring and determination beyond what most of us could even imagine. The course of human history was changed by his voyage—made better in many ways for the descendants of Europeans, made far worse in other ways for descendants of Native Americans, in the five hundred years since his glorious and dreadful landing among the gentle unknown people whom the Spaniards would so quickly enslave and slaughter.

Nothing can change what has happened, [1.] but history is what we make of what happened, and that means trying to see not just how we came to be where we are, but also where we seem to be headed. We all expect, or so I believe, that our grandchildren or great-grandchildren will steer great starships out toward worlds even more strange and magnificent than the Paradisical islands where Columbus, looking for an old world, first encountered what seemed to Europeans a new world.

We may all be very wrong: it may be that little green beings in their huge and powerful ships will land on our shores, and our science will prove too weak for their divine powers, and we earthly beings will be enslaved, tortured, exterminated in our turn. Perhaps it is worthwhile, therefore, to set down here a few thoughts about the Columbian encounter, as a way to look at future encounters—whether they happen during some glorious voyage out among other stars, or precede a sudden holocaust of humans on the Paradisical world we now inhabit, or lead to assimilation with little green beings if they should be less murderous than the Europeans proved to be. Wherever we are headed, then, here is a re-view of that Columbian encounter. It juxtaposes words from Columbus, Milton, and Shakespeare, and draws less familiar parallels—and contrasts—between Columbian, Navajo, and Osage versions of how and why we, and our nations, have come to be what we are, where we are, and who we are, on this earth.

PARADISE FOUND AND PARADISE LOST

Columbus, in his letter on his first voyage, reports that the people who came to meet him as he landed

have no religion and are not idolaters; but all believe that power and goodness dwell in the sky and they are firmly convinced that I have come from the sky. [2.]

Reading this, I could not help recalling the great lines from Paradise Lost where Milton retells the Roman myth of Vulcan, god of fire and technology: Vulcan, who had angered Jupiter, was thrown out of Heaven and brought his craft to humans, much as Columbus brought it to the "New World." Milton expected his readers to remember that the Roman gods were devils in disguise: Vulcan took the appearance of a god to seduce humans away from the worship of the true God.

Milton gave the devil his due—some of the most magnificent lines in *Paradise Lost*. He fingers Vulcan as the architect of Hell's Palace of Pandemonium (a word Milton coined to mean "city *of all the Demons*"), and pictures the fallen angels, now devils, as awed when they first enter. This brilliant technologist, this urban architect Vulcan (Milton tells us), had earlier designed the high-rises of Heaven, and we feel in the rhythm and cadences of Milton's lines all that had been lost in such a being's corruption and fall:

He [Vulcan's] hand was known
In Heaven by many a towered structure high,
Where sceptred angels held their residence
And sat as princes, whom the Supreme King
Exalted to such power, and gave to rule,
Each in his hierarchy, the orders bright.
Nor was his name unheard or unadored
In ancient Greece; and in Ausonian land [Italy]
Men called him Mulciber, and how he fell
From Heaven they fabled, thrown by angry Jove
Sheer o'er the crystal battlements: from morn
To noon he fell, from noon to dewy eve,
A summer's day, and with the setting sun
Dropped from the zenith like a falling star
On Lemnos, the Aegean isle. Thus they relate,
Erring—for he with this rebellious rout
Fell long before. 3.

Reading those lines, I remember that Columbus served the absolute monarchs of Spain, with all its romantic castles and cathedrals ("towered structures high"), and its Grand Inquisitor. He brought to the people of this hemisphere a technology and a palace-making power almost as great as (in Milton's account) Vulcan had brought first to Hell and then to Europe—and I think Columbus carried, in his Niña, Pinta, and Santa Maria, along with noble plans for a heavenly city, the ignoble politics of Pandemonium.

Columbus himself pictures the "new world" he had "discovered" as very like the oldest world of which he knew: Eden and its Garden of Paradise. He records in the logbook of his first voyage, on Sunday 21 October, what he saw as he stepped ashore on the island he would call Isabela:

The trees and plants are as green as in Andalusia in April. The singing of
small birds is so sweet that no one could ever wish to leave this place.
Flocks of parrots darken the sun and there is a marvelous variety of large
and small birds very different from our own; the trees are of many kinds,

each with its own fruit, and all have a marvelous scent. It grieves me extremely that I cannot identify them, for I am quite certain that they are all valuable and I am bringing samples of them and of the plants also. As I was walking beside one of the lagoons I saw a snake, which we killed. I am bringing it to your Highnesses. 4.

You see (Columbus marvels), I stepped from *October* onto an island, and found myself in *April's* blossoms and birdsong! Moreover, as he notes elsewhere for his Christian readers (for whom it would be a sign of the Earthly Paradise), flower, leaf and fruit here grow all at once on the same trees, not dying the seasonal death which Adam's fall had brought into the world as Europeans know it.

It is remarkable that Columbus noted the serpent's presence, that he killed it, and yet that he did not read any Christian symbolism into this. The island might resemble Eden, but Columbus was not about to suggest that he would let it remain unfallen. In fact, he was already planning how to take over this paradise, enslave its gentle inhabitants, and convert its fruitful innocence into wealth for Spain's monarchs, and a dukedom for himself and his heirs:

Should your highnesses command it all the inhabitants could be taken away to Castile or held as slaves on the island, for with fifty men we could subjugate them all and make them do what we wish...Generally it was my wish to pass no island without taking possession of it, though having annexed one it might be said that we had annexed all. 5.

He carefully notes every instance of a gold ornament on any of the natives, remarks that they *do not prize it as riches but only for its ornamental value,* observes that they are extremely generous and trusting (in these first encounters; the natives before very long saw that trust was hardly the right attitude if they wanted to keep their lives and freedom), and he sends men to search for gold at every opportunity. During his second voyage (1493-96), as his son Hernando tells us, Columbus concluded that the natives had no concept of private property:

On entering these houses, the Indians whom the Admiral brought from Isabela promptly seized anything that pleased them and the owners showed no sign of resentment. They seemed to hold all possessions in common *[emphasis mine]. Similarly, whenever any of the natives went up to a Christian, they took from him whatever they liked, in the belief that similar customs obtained among us. But they were quickly undeceived.* [6.]

Columbus had remarked, in the letter on his first voyage, as to the sexual arrangements, private property, and distribution of food among the natives:

The men are seemingly content with one woman, but their chief or king is allowed more than twenty. The women appear to work more than the men and I have not been able to find out if they have private property. As far as I could see whatever a man had was shared among all the rest and this particularly applies to food. [7.]

In other words, Columbus *did not notice any instances of people going hungry while others had plenty or more than enough.* There were no homeless, there were no hungry, there were no poor when he arrived, so far as he could see.

It would be naive to claim that the actual condition of all the natives was so Edenic as the passages quoted above seem meant to suggest. Columbus, like all the later explorers, had to raise funds for exploring, and therefore had to be a master of public relations and hype—as we see in his log, his letters, and his son's account of his voyages, where Columbus keeps assuring readers that there are fantastic amounts of gold on the very next island, which he has not yet managed to explore. His praise of the unbelievable fertility apparent in the lush growth of useful and delicious plants, his harping on the docility of the natives, were meant to help win further funding, so as to recruit more soldiers, laborers, craftsmen, and clergy, to turn this Eden into a Christian empire, with himself as its viceroy.

CANNIBALS AND THE "MIRROR OF ALL CHRISTIAN KINGS"

So Columbus deliberately gilded the lily he found. But he does show us, growing around that lily, lots of poison ivy. Or, to put it more plainly, he discovered that there were cannibals on some islands, and some definitely "fallen" behavior: raiding, abduction, castration, rape, looting. If reading Columbus sometimes reminds me of reading Milton, at other times some of his first-hand descriptions of behavior among the natives of this "New World" remind me of scenes from Shakespeare. About the Caribs, for instance, the physican named Dr. Chanca (whom Ferdinand and Isabela sent with Columbus on his second voyage) wrote:

> *These people raid the other islands and carry off all the women they can take, especially the young and beautiful, whom they keep as servants and concubines...These women say that they are treated with a cruelty that seems incredible. The Caribs eat the male children that they have by them...They castrate the boys that they capture and use them as servants until they are men. Then they kill and eat them.* [8.]

As Dr. Chanca says, "The customs of these Carib people are beastly." I certainly agree—and yet his words remind me of a passage in Shakespeare's *Henry the Fifth*, in which King Henry warns the French citizens of the town of Harfleur, which he is besieging, of what will happen to them if they continue to resist his siege. (The incident dates historically from 1415, during the Hundred Years' War between England and France over who should be king of France.) Shakespeare presents King Henry as the "mirror of all Christian kings," a very interesting view since in the third act of the play Henry tells the mayor of Harfleur that if the town surrenders its inhabitants will be treated leniently, but if they have to be defeated by siege then the victorious English soldiers will behave very much like the Caribs whom Dr. Chanca found so beastly:

> *For as I am a soldier,*
> *A name that in my thoughts becomes me best,*
> *If I begin the battery once again,*
> *The gates of mercy shall be all shut up,*
> *And the fleshed soldier, rough and hard of heart,*
> *In liberty of bloody hand shall range*
> *With conscience wide as hell, mowing like grass*
> *Your fresh fair virgins and your flowering infants.*
> *What is it to me, if you yourselves are cause,*
> *If your pure maidens fall into the hand*
> *Of hot and forcing violation?*

Take pity of your town and of your people,

Whiles yet my soldiers are in my command—

If not, why, in a moment look to see

The blind and bloody soldier with foul hand

Defile the locks of your shrill-shrieking daughters,

Your fathers taken by their silver beards

And their most reverend heads dashed to the walls;

Your naked infants spitted upon pikes,

While the mad mothers with their howls confused

Do break the clouds, as did the wives of Jewry

At Herod's bloody-hunting slaughtermen.

What say you? Will you yield, and this avoid?

Or guilty in defence *[emphasis mine], be thus destroyed?* 9.

It is clear to anyone reading Dr. Chanca's account of how the Caribs raided, murdered, raped, looted, and kidnapped that their acts match fairly closely the description given by King Henry of what his soldiers will just "naturally" do, if the mayor of Harfleur should try to defend his town against Henry's invading army. King Henry, it may be said, is invading only to validate his claim that he is the true King of France. However, if the mayor of Harfleur accepted Henry's claim, the reigning French king could behead the mayor as a traitor. The rules of European warfare were very orderly but not very pleasant for those in the mayor's position. The powerful can do anything and justify it, but the weak had better do whatever the most powerful say, or the second most powerful will destroy them. If the weak wait to see who is most powerful, as the mayor would like to do, they can be beheaded (and worse!) for waiting.

Surely the gentle Arawaks, caught between Columbus and the Caribs, would have recognized in that besieged mayor of Harfleur and his citizens their fellow hostages to a threatening savage power. Surely, too, they would have understood that when Dr. Chanca exclaimed that the Carib customs were *beastly*, the good Doctor was looking into a mirror—or, as Shakespeare put it, looking at *the mirror of all Christian kings.*

In the Fast Track of the Columbus 500

The usual next step in an essay on Columbus would be to turn from old negative to new positive. After all, I sit writing this on a word processor, a splendid product of European (or, in 1992, Asiatic?) technology—despite my having just compared the introducer of such skills to a devil hurled from heaven for inventing gunpowder. And I live comfortably in a green suburb, two streets from the serenely expensive university where I have tenure. I write in the English language, mind-crafted over thousands of years and given to me at birth, at ease in the most powerful and one of the freest nations on earth. The shapers of this nation—heirs of Columbus—worked to make better living conditions, both material and spiritual, than were possible in the "old" Europe. All this, as an American citizen, I most gratefully acknowledge.

And in the OneEyed Ford*

Yet within this bountiful nation millions of humans are less well cared for than were the island natives where Columbus first landed. Homeless and hungry people cannot get good medical care because they have no money, insurance, status. We live in a good society—but good mostly for those with "good" educations, the right skin color, friends, banks.

Nor is it only humans who suffer more in this our great nation than did the natives in their small islands. Our relatives also ache: animals and plants, the air, the water, earth herself. The electricity that brilliantly lights New York City is not generated on Manhattan itself: rather, out in "the sticks," sulfurous fires send their acid and cinders up into the lungs and flowers of every living creature downwind from "towered structures high." From this burning and pollution, set on the green prairie or in the dusty desert, comes the power that lights our thousand-storied buildings, our neon jungles, our living rooms. If a Phoenix glitters and bathes itself in snowmelt waters there in Arizona, we can see from our jetplanes the fouled nest it sprang from, the smoke and scars of Black Mesa coalpits in the Navajo Nation: the price paid by Navajo, Hopi, and all of us, for our "enlightenment."

---

* A "OneEyed Ford" is an old jalopy with one good headlight, celebrated in contemporary American Indian songs. The Chippewa poet Diane Burns has a collection of poems called *Riding the OneEyed Ford*.

We also suck other veins for such god-juice, our fix of electrons that seem to alter time and space in spilling the long-dead music of Beethoven, or the far-off wars of the Middle East, into our living rooms. From deep within infinitesimal atomic nuclei we draw the power we need, then spit out the glowing waste it makes, bury it deep in the future for grandchildren to step upon—even while sun and wind and water wait like angels for us to turn their power into a light that would leave fewer ashes and less oily smoke than the flames of Kuwait, fewer oil-fouled shores and sea creatures than the tankers of Exxon, less leukemia and abortion than the eruptions of Chernobyl.

In short, we still have not clearly improved on what Columbus found when he stepped ashore to meet those who had cared for this continent until then. If and when I see a United States where the hungry all are fed, where differences in ability, income and race are not used to divide us into a wealthy and overfed few on the one hand, and a hungry, ill-fed, ill-housed many on the other, *then* I will agree that the coming of Columbus was not a bad thing. And if I see Indian nations free and healthy again, I'll be happy to celebrate!

HOW THE OSAGE NATION CAME FROM THE SKY

But we have focused thus far on Columbus and what the Europeans have made of this continent, making only brief mention of how well the Indians seem to have managed *before* Columbus got here. It might be thought that such good management was "just natural," that the Indians had no consciousness of ordering themselves or achieving harmony with the world they lived in. Let us, then, compare Adam's apple with Montezuma's papaya, so to speak: let us see how two pre-Columbian societies conceived and dedicated themselves (as Lincoln phrased it) to the proposition that all men are created equal—and to the nobler proposition that all beings are our equals. These matters are dealt with in the Creation Stories—those parts of sacred tribal histories that tell how Osages came to be Osage, Navajos to be Navajo, in this very world, among its very creatures and conditions.

During the Osage Naming Ceremony [10.], for instance, each of the tribal clan-representatives present would recite that clan's version of the Osage

Creation Story, as a way of affirming that the child being named was descended from those first beings who came into this world as founders of the Osage Nation. These beings, in the Osage story, came from the stars, at a time after this world had been created as the Waters, and the Earth, and the Sky. At that time, those who would become the Osage Nation decided to come to this world. Being sensible and cautious people, they sent ahead many scouts to find out how they might live and become an enduring people in the world as it had been created and shaped. Each of the scouts traveled ahead, and each met a sacred being who offered help in finding the right ways to live in this world. These sacred beings included the Eagle, the Red Cedar, the Buffalo, Elk, Black Bear, and others; each of these then became the guide for a "clan" or "gens" of the Osage Nation. In each meeting, the sacred being said the same thing: *If you make your bodies of me, you will live to see old age, and live into the peaceful days.*

The Osages saw human and "animal" relations differently from the way these are viewed in the biblical accounts, which Columbus would have known. In the Bible, Adam and Eve are in one version created together in God's image; in another, Eve is made from Adam's rib, after the animals have been created.[11.] The animals are not only subordinate, but subservient, to humans. In contrast, the Osages tell of meeting the animals of this world in a sacred dimension, before actually descending into this world—and they are given by the animals the wisdom to live in this world in a good way that will allow them to endure into "the peaceful days," which implies more than "old age."

The Osage account has profound wisdom. As our "animal scientists" continue to discover, animals do show us how to live in this world. They came into this world long before we did and, as we are discovering, some of their ways of sensing its phenomena, of finding their way around among its powers and dangers, anticipate and rival our high-tech devices and procedures. If, for instance, we ask how Columbus managed to sail across the Atlantic Ocean, we know that he had a magnetic compass, something fairly new in navigational technology, recorded from European sources of the late twelfth century A.D., perhaps used in the East about that time also, according to encyclopedias. He steered by the sun and stars, but when they were not visible, he could steer by his compass. We are just beginning to understand a little of how animals map their world and what they use to navigate within it: in a June 1991 *National Geographic*, for instance, I read that pigeons

> *see ultraviolet light and hear extremely low-frequency sound...From anywhere in the United States,...[their] keen ears hear a volcano erupting in Java or winds swirling around the Andes.* [12.]

It may be that tiny specks of ferrite in the pigeon's brain are linked to sensory nerves and allow it to "see" magnetic lines of force; its ability to see light-polarization helps it when the sun is hidden by clouds. Our nuclear submarines under the Arctic ice are, perhaps, kept aware of what is going on in Washington or Moscow by the kind of "ultra-low sound" that alerts pigeons to the volcanoes of Java, the surf patterns of California or North Carolina, the thunderstorms of Colorado, the tornadoes on their way to the dovecote. [13.] Watch the birds, and forecast the storms for the weekend? Well, perhaps the Indians were right to respect what animals can teach us.

In the Osage Creation Story, which was recited as part of the Naming Ceremony and therefore was heard many times by assembled families as their children were being "brought into" the tribal society, we see animals as partners, teachers, and helpers, welcoming us into this world, giving us ways to survive and prevail in our earthly lives. Perhaps when the Arawaks thought Columbus "came from the sky," and welcomed him to this world that was new to him, they had some such belief in mind: a new group of beings, in those three ships, was coming to this world, and those already here could welcome and show them how to survive.

One more point has always come up whenever we discuss the Osage Naming Ceremony in my classes on American Indian literature: is it only "mythmaking" to say that humans come from the stars? Is it more "factually accurate" to say that humans are made out of this earth we live on, as is said in the Hebrew Creation Story? To these questions I respond with another: where does this earth come from, if not the stars? Not just ordinary stars either, but from supernovas, in whose explosions are produced all the heavier elements in our human bodies; so if we are formed of the dust of the ground, that dust is also star-stuff. And as for this planet Earth, it is certainly among the stars, is it not? We *do* come "from the stars," just as we *do* come "from the earth." The old Hebrews got it right; so did the old Osages. Thinking about the "old myths" can perhaps have its humbling uses. It may well be that myths are like the stars: we see by their light, even though they may have "died" centuries ago.

HOW THE NAVAJO NATION CAME FROM THE EARTH

The Osages are hardly the only Indian nation to build such wisdom into their stories. Consider, for instance, the Navajo Creation Story, and particularly three points which "mainstream" readers might ponder. First is the way the Navajo storytellers have evidently added to their earlier "Gambler" stories one that deals with the Europeans who had by then conquered Mexico; in this we see how flexible the Navajo "canon" of sacred stories could be, allowing them to present and comment on the "new" people on the continent. A second point is what the Navajo can tell us about sexual relations. And third is something we need to consider when we think of eliminating evils from our world. (In discussing these matters, I ask for tolerance from the Navajo people; my knowledge of Navajo ways is very limited, and the following remarks rely mostly on Paul Zolbrod's *Diné Bahanè, The Navajo Creation Story*. [14.]

WHY THE GAMBLER WAS SENT TO MEXICO

The powerful Gambler first appears well into the Navajo Creation Story, after the people have come up from the First World through the Second, Third, and Fourth into the Fifth World in which we live. At that time, "a gambling god" descends into the midst of the Pueblo people and challenges them to "all sorts of games," which he always wins. [15.] He soon has won all the possessions of the Pueblo villagers, forces them to build a race track and an arena for his gambling games, and reduces them all to slave laborers.

Until then, the ancestors of the Navajo had remained aloof from this disaster, tending their own affairs. But one day, the kindly Talking God comes to them and tells a young Navajo man that the Gambler has just won the shells which are the greatest treasures of the Pueblo peoples, kept by them for the Sun, and the Gambler refuses to return these treasures to the Sun.

Now the Sun and other Holy People are going to assemble in the mountains and decide what to do about this Gambler. The young Navajo man is invited to attend and there finds that the animals who are pets of the Pueblo people, but whom the Gambler now "owns," have come to the meeting, "unhappy at being someone else's property."

The Navajo conspires with the gods and animals to outwit the Gambler. With the young Navajo fronting for them, and using in turn the powers of the various gods and animals, they win everything back from the Gambler. When he curses gods and humans, they tell him:

> *Remember that you bet your very self, and admit that you have lost...You are not one of the Holy People...You may have gained power over some of your own kind. But you have no such power over us. Not here in this world.* [16.]

At this, the god Wind draws a magic bow, places the Gambler in it like an arrow, and shoots him into the sky, the realm of the mischief-making god Begochidi. When the Gambler tells his sad story to this god, he gets sympathy—so much, that Begochidi decides to make the Gambler rich and powerful once again.

Here is where we see the Navajo have added to their original Creation Story's section on the Gambler an episode that deals with the post-Columbus situation. In this addition, Begochidi makes the Gambler rich again by creating for him a whole new people, the Mexicans, as well as the domestic animals brought to America by the Europeans: sheep, burros, pigs, goats, and horses. Begochidi then sends the Gambler and these newly created beings back into our Fifth World—not to Pueblo and Navajo country, this time, but to "a place far to the south," Mexico:

> *Having died there soon after his return, he dwells there to this very day as god of...the Mexican people.* [17.]

Two things strike me about this Gambler episode. One is its socioeconomic point, that *it is possible, but socially destructive, for one person to amass great wealth and enslave other people—and that this should be stopped by communal action.* Second is that this point *is carefully turned to apply sharply to Europeans*, since the Gambler is not destroyed (in the post-

Columbus version), but is sent back to be the God of the European-created country of Mexico. The Navajo thinkers, it seems, decided that while the robber baron mentality is a bad thing among Pueblo and Navajo people, it is well suited to the European colonial society. Not only, then, has the Navajo Creation Story been adapted at this point to take account of the coming of the Europeans, it offers a shrewd and realistic comment on the social values and dynamics of those Europeans. It identifies, if we want to draw a New Testament parallel, Mammon as the God of the European society, and suggests just as Jesus did that it is sometimes reasonable to "make friends with the Mammon of iniquity." I wonder what Navajo storytellers made of that part of the Christian Gospels?

MAKING SEX BEAUTIFUL—BUT NOT TOO BEAUTIFUL

So the drive for money and possessions and power was firmly put by the Navajo Creation Story into its proper place. But what about the sexual drives, and social relations between men and women? On these matters, the Navajo account seems much fuller than what Columbus would have found in his Bible. Adam and Eve were commanded to be fruitful and multiply, but God said little about the proper relationships between men and women, in either of the two Biblical narratives of how humans were created. [18.] After laying down divine policy—to populate the earth—God seems not to have legislated the details. It was left up to Adam and Eve as to how to implement this policy. Commentators divide on just when they began implementing (some say before, some say after the Fall), but it is clear that they succeeded. On the other hand, alert readers might notice that the biblical text is silent about the inevitable implication that, for a good while, such populating must have been done by incest.

The Navajo narrative, in contrast, is outspoken and detailed. Once First Man and First Woman had been created (the male from a white ear of corn, the female from a yellow one), the gods had a shelter of brushwood made and told them to live together in it as man and wife. Of this union, five pairs of twins were born. The first pair were hermaphrodites, the other four sets each had one male and one female. For a time, the twin pairs lived together as husbands and wives but, growing ashamed of this incest, they found spouses among the Mirage People. First Woman, seeing this change, was glad, but worried that people would find it too easy to renounce marriage and take new spouses. She thought marriage should be made very attractive, because there is a great deal of work that humans must do and *it is best if they marry and divide the work between them.* [19.] To ensure that harmony might prevail, marriages should last. Meditating on how to achieve this end, First Woman did not impose negative commandments, nor did she act hastily. Instead, she waited until people had invented farming, irrigating, pottery, farm tools, hunting and hunting ceremonies, and ways to make clothing. Then she went to work:

> *She fashioned a penis of turquoise. Then she rubbed loose cuticle from a woman's breast and mixed it up with yucca fruit, which she put inside the turquoise penis...Next she made a vagina of white shell. Into the vagina she placed a clitoris of red shell. Then she rubbed loose cuticle from a man's breast and mixed it with yucca fruit, which she placed in the clitoris. And she combined herbs with various kinds of water and placed that mixture deep inside the vagina. That way pregnancy would occur.* [20.]

> *She then not only arranged for both penis and vagina to experience orgasm, she carefully adjusted the intensity of first and second orgasms for each, until she was sure that men and women would learn to care for each other. They would be eager to have children,...share the labor evenly, and... each more willingly tend to the other's needs.* [21.]

Even after such thoughtful arrangement, however, things nearly got botched by the intervention of another figure: Coyote, the powerful "trickster" figure. Coyote had come into existence soon after First Woman made the sexual arrangements just described; in fact, he appeared during puberty ceremonies in which elders were giving a penis to a boy and a vagina to a girl who had come of age. The people at the ceremony noticed that the sky was swooping down to embrace the earth, and just where sky met earth, Coyote and Badger sprang out of the ground. [22.] Coyote at once came over to watch the puberty ceremony, but in his typical way he decided that he could improve the arrangements, and he proceeded to make the sexual organs a great deal more attractive. First Woman saw that this "improvement" would cause men and women to be too easily drawn together, so she ordered them to wear clothes whenever in company with other people.

What might Columbus and his men have thought, had they been able somehow to hear and understand this narrative of the way divine powers, with human cooperation, and despite an impish intervention, could integrate the powerful forces of sex and possessive desires into an ordered human society? Would some of those Spanish soldiers have been tempted to think these "Indians" *did* have religion, and powers of social reason, after all? Would they have thought that perhaps this story's account of the "deadly sins" of lust and greed was at least worth comparing with the traditional Christian account of them?

ON SLAYING MONSTERS AND DISPOSING OF TOXIC WASTE

Finally, the Navajo Creation Story has a very interesting slant on how to deal with some dangerous by-products of human activities. It seems that despite First Woman's excellent arrangements and good judgment, she and First Man had a fearsome quarrel. First Man had brought deer meat for dinner, but after eating heartily, First Woman belched and thanked her vagina for the delicious meal. First Man, annoyed, asked if she thought her vagina was the great hunter that had brought home this delicious dinner. Why yes, she said—were it not for the vagina, no men would do anything. First Man said, Well! Maybe you women think you can live without us men? The quarrel escalated until First Man just walked out. Next day all the men went over the river, leaving the women to themselves—and the women just said, Good riddance!

At first each group considered that it was doing just fine, and they taunted each other across the river. (One might imagine how this story would be useful in Navajo domestic situations later!) As time went on, however, the needs and difficulties springing from the separation overwhelmed them, and with encouragement from various beings, the men and women got back together. However, a great flood drove them from the Fourth World in which these things had happened, up into the Fifth (our present) World. Even after reaching this safety, dire consequences dogged them, in the form of monsters begotten by sexual self-abuse while the sexes were separated. It was with these monsters that disorder came into the world, and the monsters grew and began to ambush and devour the people, who were reduced to a small number.

At that time, First Man journeyed to the top of Spruce Mountain, and there obtained divine help: the gods brought into existence the powerful figures of Changing Woman and White Shell Woman. Changing Woman then had a son by the Sun, and White Shell Woman had a son by the Water. Grown up, these sons became the Monster Slayers who, by courage, many ruses, and help from Changing Woman and the Sun, destroy the deadly monsters. 23.

At this point the Navajo "slant" on how to deal with such evils becomes (to me) most fascinating. When each of the monsters is killed, the Monster-Slaying Twins see to it that *something good is made of its corpse.* One reason they do this may be hinted at, in the story, when their father the Sun—whose help they need—makes them understand that the monster they are about to kill is the Sun's own child, and therefore is half-brother to the elder of the Monster-Slaying Twins. This implies, surely, that whatever evils human beings have to "wipe out" are likely to be "part of us," instead of being truly "aliens."24.

How explicit the story is may be seen in an instance or two. When the Twins and the Sun kill the Giant Monster *Ye'iitsoh,* chips of his flint armor go flying. Seeing this, the elder Twin says, "Let us gather those flint flakes. Our people can use them." Agreeing, the other Twin says: "That way we can turn Ye'iitsoh's evil into something good."25. Similar use was made of the Bird Monsters, whose children were made into eagles and owls as they now exist, and later (in an adventure with Bat Woman) their feathers became all the different small birds as we know them. 26.

I see strong moral implications here. First, *we are related to the evils we must destroy: they come from our own behavior.* Second, *these evils can be turned to good things.* It is worth noting here that not all the good things would seem particularly good to people outside the Navajo ways. The children of the Cliff Monster, for instance, become the carrion-eating

Vultures, while the children of the Monsters Who Kill With Their Eyes become the Whippoorwills, to whom the Monster-Slayer says,

> *It will be your destiny to make things sound beautiful. It will be your fate to make the world a happy place when darkness falls, [reassuring] all who hear you that the Sun will rise in the morning and bring forth a new day.* [27.]

The Navajo are no Pollyannas, but they seem to have relied less on negative commandments or fear of punishment than on the belief in achieving harmony by positive actions. Their stories touch directly on the fight which we as post-Columbians are now waging to tame certain monsters who are ambushing us in "our" world: Strip-Mining Monsters, Nuclear Waste Monsters, Urban Sprawl and Social Alienation, and Racial Fear Monsters.

In short, the Vulcans in Milton's myth of how things got into such bad shape, and the Monsters of the Navajo version, are always out there to be dealt with by those of us into whose world they have fallen, setting the fires that now blaze on all the continents of this earth, and sowing the ashes that will choke us if we do not turn them into something good. The stories of post-Columbians and of pre-Columbians are all vital to our understanding of where we are in 1992, five hundred years after Columbus dropped from the zenith like a falling star on that Caribbean isle, whose Indian name we will never know, and "enlightened" two continents in his shining path.

NOTES

1. I wonder what might have been the social and political situation in North and Central America, had Europeans only been precisely five hundred years "behind schedule" in their social and technical development, so that Columbus might have landed on that Caribbean island on October 12, 1992. What might have been the populations, social structures, and technologies of the Central American nations—or, indeed, of the native peoples of what is now the southeastern United States? When DeSoto passed through in the 1500s, an extensive chiefdom called *Coosa* controlled a region more than two hundred miles long in the present states of Tennessee, Georgia, and Alabama; see Marvin T. Smith, "Indian Responses to European Contact: The Coosa Example," in *First Encounters*, ed. J. T. Milanich and S. Milbrath (University of Florida Press, 1989), pp. 135-49.

2. J. M. Cohen, ed. and translator, *The Four Voyages of Columbus* (Penguin, 1969), p. 118.

3. John Milton, *Paradise Lost,* ed. Scott Elledge (Norton, 1975), Book One, lines 732-48.

4. Cohen, *Four Voyages,* p. 70.

5. Ibid., pp 58, 60.

6. Ibid., p. 161.

7. Ibid., p. 121.

8. Ibid., p. 136-67.

9. Henry V, ed. Gary Taylor (Oxford University Press, 1984), Act III, Sc. iii, lines 81-122 (some lines omitted here). The description of Henry V as "the mirror of all Christian kings" is given by the chorus before Act II (line 6).

10. The Osage Tribe: Two Versions of the Child-Naming Rite. Washington, D.C.: Bureau of American Ethnology Annual Report No. 43, 1924-25, pp. 23-264. I have discussed this in "Traditional Osage Naming Ceremonies: Entering the Circle of Being," in A. Krupat and B. Swann, *Recovering the Word* (University of California Press, 1987), pp. 446-68.

11. The "first version" of Eve's creation by God is in Genesis 1: 26-27, where God made both man and woman at the same time, in his own image, male and female. The "second version" is in Genesis 2: 7-25, where God formed man out of the dust of the ground, put him (Adam) into the Garden of Eden, and there anesthetized Adam and took a rib from his side, of which God fashioned Eve.

12. Michael E. Long, "Secrets of Animal Navigation," *National Geographic* 179 (6) (June 1991): pp. 80, 95.

13. Ibid., p. 97.

14. Paul Zolbrod, *Diné Bahanè, The Navajo Creation Story*. University of New Mexico Press, 1984. Cited below as D.B.

15. D.B., p. 99.

16. D.B., p. 110.

17. D.B., p. 112.

18. Of course the commentators on the biblical accounts have a great deal to say, but the Bible itself is very brief. Eve is said by Adam, after she has been fashioned from his rib, to be "bone of my bones, and flesh of my flesh: she shall be called Woman, because she was taken out of Man. Therefore shall a man leave his father and his mother, and shall cleave unto his wife: and they shall be one flesh" (Genesis 2: 23-5). After the Fall, God tells Eve that (as punishment, it seems) he will "greatly multiply" her sorrow and her conception, adding: "Thy desire shall be to thy husband, and he shall rule over thee" (Genesis 2: 16). These passages seem to say only that the husband/wife relation takes precedent over the husband/parents relation, and that wives must submit to being ruled by husbands.

19. D.B., p. 53.

20. D.B., p. 55.

21. D.B., p. 56.

22. D.B., pp. 56-57.

23. D.B., pp. 58-78, 94-99, 171-269.

24. D.B., p. 211

25. D.B., p. 220.

26. D.B., pp. 235-36.

27. D.B., p. 247.

Ray A. Young Bear

Ray A. Young Bear, born 1950, is a lifetime resident of the Mesquakie (Red Earth) Tribal Settlement in central Iowa. His poems have appeared in many anthologies and magazines, including *American Poetry Review, Virginia Quarterly Review, Kenyon Review,* and *Harper's Anthology of Twentieth-Century Native American Poetry.* He has also published three books of poems, *Winter of the Salamander, The Invisible Musician,* and *Black Eagle Child.*

JOURNAL OF A MESQUAKIE POET: NOTES LEADING TO 500 YEARS AFTER

by Ray A. Young Bear

In the twenty years or so that I have been involved with poetry readings and visiting artist/lecturer residencies here in Iowa and the greater Midwest—an occupation which never ceases to astound me in light of my Mesquakie ("People of the Red Earth") roots—I have discovered that young people in this "advanced" nation of ours are extremely fortunate to know anything when it comes to Native Americans and their tragic history.

Since Native Americans have much to do with who I am because of my tribal affiliation, this certainty of young people not knowing and perhaps never knowing enough about my ancestry hits me on a personal level.

We have been apprised that, academically, Iowa students are among the best when compared to others, but I find their knowledge about Native Americans is embarrassingly next to zero. Yet I suspect it is no better in Azusa, California, or Rome, New York. While these students are fully aware of our existence, such knowledge is often weighed down with stereotypes. Take for example the range of questions I received this past year from elementary and high school students:

"Mr. Young Bear, do you live in a tepee?" "Have you ever scalped anyone?" "Do you wear feathers?" "Did you ride into town today on a horse?" "Do you own a bow and arrow and have you ever hunted buffalo?" "How does it feel to be an Indian?"

Knowing these questions were quite serious, I usually responded with light-hearted but truthful answers that went something like this:

"Dear Child. . . . First of all, just like you and everyone else here, I live in a house and enjoy the conveniences of modern life. I have indoor plumbing, a VCR, TV, stereo, computer, and so forth. The ways you and I live are in many respects the same. It is our beliefs that are different.

"Secondly, the tepee dwellings of which you speak belong primarily to the Northern Plains tribes, like the Sioux, the Crow, and the Blackfeet. But contrary to what you've been taught, those people don't live in tepees anymore. Long ago they used to.

"As for scalping, I don't believe in buying or re-selling rock concert or sports tickets at exorbitant prices.

"As for the donning of feathers, do you see any on me?" I ask, holding assuredly to the lapels of my suit or vest. The classroom often breaks into nervous laughter before I mention that ceremonial regalia is worn for special occasions only, and compare it to church-going "Sunday Best" clothing. It should be noted that often a sponsor will audaciously suggest I arrive in "traditional garb," which I will not honor lest I perpetuate such a narrow-minded view of Native Americans. I wouldn't think of doing the converse, of asking anyone to wear their *klompens,* wooden shoes, or Viking furs unless that was their sole *folkloristische* occupation.

"And about my horse?" I continue. "I hate to ruin grand impressions, but my horse is Japanese-made, a 1987 Toyota Tercel with close to 100,000 miles on the odometer. It doesn't eat hay . . . nor does it make the mess afterwards.

"And my only association with bows and arrows, I am sorry to say, came in my childhood via rubber-tipped arrows and bull's-eye targets.

"As for hunting buffalo, I've never had the pleasure. You see, your forefathers wiped them out." The tempo of the classroom laughter will subside but rise again as I explain, "But I imagine if I ever met a snorting buffalo with its horns gleaming widely in the sunlight somewhere in the cornfields, I'd run like HELL, and I'm sure you'd run alongside me."

"Nowadays—and I don't think you'll be too surprised to learn this—we hunt at the same place your parents hunt. Which is where? Yes, you've got it—the local supermarket. My wife, Stella, and I crouch in the aisles of the meat and produce sections like this," and I break into an exaggerated pantomime, "hunting with our delicate senses for the freshest and cheapest items possible.

"And how does it feel to be Indian? That may well be the most important question of the day. Let me ask you a question in return. Hopefully, your answer will be the same as mine. Do you enjoy being a human being?"

Informing students that Native Americans live very much like other Americans, enjoying the same pleasures, or living the same lives of torment, is never without obstacles. The chance of students digesting and keeping such information when presented through laughter and with startling insights is greater than through outright didacticism. To do this, I use a little brain jarring, mixed with a hefty dose of humor, art, and music, incorporating autobiographical elements into my cultural and creative arts presentations.

When I use poetry and bilingual/bicultural books to narrate and juxtapose tribal life past and present, students are often astounded to know we share similar pleasures, including Red Lobster's ocean delicacies and Casey Kasem's Top 40 radio program. Once the shards of old misconceptions have flown out the window, I tie the connections stronger by confessing that, like many non-Indians, I too am hopelessly mesmerized with the award-winning pop singer Mariah Carey. If I can leave a classroom knowing I have eradicated at least some of the vestiges of frontier mentality, I will feel successful. If a teacher later records, "More poetry should have been read, as was the original intent," I will shrug and smile. Poetry can easily take a back seat if I believe I am the first—and possibly last—Native American the students will ever see, hear, and talk to.

As one of few Native American spokesmen within a 300-mile radius, correcting misconceptions about Native Americans can be a God-awful burden, especially when the educational system turns out to be the mute culprit. A crucial chapter in the American saga seems to be untold. We must soon move toward the proper and judicious presentation of facts. It is rare to meet educators who go beyond the three Rs. Obviously the trend among most is to concentrate on subjects needed for modern survival, which is their prerogative. But they then teach Indian-related subjects as they themselves were taught, which is somewhat outdated.

Fortunately, a handful of elite teachers choose to enlighten students of a horrendous epoch most prefer to avoid. These are the few who digress from the glorification of Thanksgiving via paper cut-outs of Pilgrims and Indians having an ancient cookout. Although to hear fifth and sixth graders discuss early tribes who received "contaminated grain and spoiled meat" and "blanket gifts infested with the smallpox germ" is a dramatic departure, simply knowing of past atrocities is meaningless unless a keen sense of remorse results. I say this because any discussion of the past nowadays is, instead, usually met with apathy. (This bridge-burning attitude is a carry-over from those European immigrants who wanted to melt indistinguishably into the pot.) Within some segments of the older populace, the typical response is, "We're tired of feeling guilty. Let bygones be bygones. If it hadn't been us, it would've been someone else." Yet that doesn't mean the first incidence of germ warfare via blanket "gifts" or the U.S. government assistance programs in the 1800s that provided contaminated grain and spoiled meats to Native Americans should not be discussed. If anything, these verities should become vital components in the interpretation of American history. But as long as this arm's-length detachment is held, other atrocities will be committed throughout the next century.

The long drives taken during the school year have left an indelible impression upon my work and consciousness. They have allowed me time to reflect on my talks about my poetry and Mesquakie background. Questions surface, dive, and resurface as the rural landscape whizzes by my car window.

Just how important is it to share such information with these young people? Should I assume the storyteller/messenger role that I first saw in my grandmother, the person who shaped my world view via mythology and spirituality? Or should I just stick to fundamentals?

When my great-great grandfather, Mamwiwanike, initiated the monumental purchase by the Mesquakie people of central Iowa land in 1856, his sole purpose was to establish a homeland for his people and those to be born afterward. To ensure the welfare and future of the Mesquakie Nation, there was a momentary acquiescence to the Euro-American value system. In exchange for cash Mamwiwanike was given a deed, a document, a piece of paper with black markings that indicated ownership of said property.

This transaction between tribe and state may be the only one of its kind. The intent, of course, was to provide a place where Mesquakie progeny could live in solitude, protected with invisible barriers from the wa be ski na me ska ta, white-skinned person.

Over 130 years have passed, and thanks to the divine wisdom of the boy-chieftain, the Mesquakie today have the distinction of being known for their tenacious beliefs. This tenacity accounts for our original language, culture, and religion still being intact. But all has not been without conflict and some loss. Heated, clan-dividing debates have raged as to what aspects of Euro-American society we should accept or reject, what to fence in and what to fence out. This is where I come in, a descendant of both the conservative and progressive factions, asking questions.

When academic studies are no longer done to determine how much we have lost and regained of our former selves, and when cultural barometers note that our tribal myths and ceremonies have successfully withstood centuries of genocide, our survival will be attributed to spirituality. But how does one report that five hundred years after Columbus the Red Earth People are basically unchanged? For clarity and to promote better understanding between peoples, should this achievement be taught?

My heart tells me that if the fundamentals of Native American history and culture aren't part of the classroom curriculum, we will continue to be portrayed in a limitless array of disturbing, degrading, and puzzling caricatures. (The Washington Redskins and the Cleveland Indians pop immediately onto the cerebral screen, along with the University of Illinois' Chief Illiniwek mascot.)

It is no surprise many schools inadvertently perpetuate romantic images of tepees, feathers, buffalos, and the like. I have no trouble with this stylized approach as long as it includes an in-depth section on contemporary Native American society. Admittedly, this is a hefty request, but when Mrs. Pinkston cannot go beyond the classroom tepees and fluorescent tempera-coated dioramas, the chance of a childhood introduction turning lopsided is increased tenfold. When laminated talking-skin drawings do no more than collect dust in the hallways, a child is left with incomplete and clouded images of "Indians." As a result, wrong impressions that remain for a lifetime are born. Add to this heap the small-town entrepreneur who sells "[Tribal Name] Burgers" (after a neighboring Indian community) and the corporate bigwigs who use "Tribal Names" on their exclusive merchandise. Our identity has been grossly misused and distorted by a country that has yet to recognize its errors.

Instead of thrashing about helplessly in the waves of the Ocean of Perpetual Malignment, I conclude it is not the fault of these innocent students nor their teachers and administrators for not knowing and perhaps never knowing enough about my ancestry. But to isolate where this misunderstanding began should be a matter of priority, for it inevitably touches upon the righteous attitudes of government and politics.

In the autumn of 1990, when area educators issued "Let's hope and pray the Persian Gulf crisis doesn't lead to war" statements at conferences and high school government classes, I was among those most pessimistic—and rightly so. "With the Native American as a monumental example, why should the United States stop short of Iraq?" I asked rhetorically, noting that the seek, befriend, steal, and destroy pattern was established centuries before at the expense of my ancestors. "That is why the word P-O-G-R-O-M exists in Webster's dictionary," I said, knowing very well a mother hen or two would cluck contemptuously and attempt to spread wings over ears. But I raised my voice. "*Pogrom* is a noun which means 'an organized slaughter of a racial or religious minority.'"

All of this leads me to speculate that while much of the hoopla scheduled for October 12, 1992, will focus on political and technological achievements of America, no one can underline firmly enough the inexcusable disrespect for humanity that has taken place. And in one way or another we are all caught in the middle, stagnating.

Paula Gunn Allen, born 1939, is of Laguna Pueblo/Lakota Native American, Scots-Irish, and Lebanese-American descent. She currently is professor of English at the University of California, Los Angeles. She was awarded the Native American Prize for Literature in 1990, and her anthology of short stories, Spider Woman's Granddaughters, was awarded the American Book Award and the Susan Koppleman Award. She has received a post-doctoral minorities scholars fellowship from the National Research Council–Ford Foundation, a post-doctoral fellowship from the Institute of American Cultures at UCLA, and an NEA writer's grant.

Allen has published seven volumes of poetry (most recently, *Skins and Bones*); the novel *The Woman Who Owned the Shadows*; a collection of her essays, *The Sacred Hoop: Recovering the Feminine in American Indian Traditions*; and two anthologies, *Studies in American Indian Literature*, and *Spider Woman's Granddaughters: Native American Women's Traditional and Short Stories.*

Lee Francis (*Hapanyi Wastch*) is an educator of Laguna/Sioux Native American and Lebanese descent. He is a member of the National Congress of American Indians as well as of the National Ethnic Studies Association. He has served as director of the American Indian Intensive Learning Academy at California State University Long Beach, associate director of the educational opportunity program at San Francisco State University, and as special assistant to two U.S. senators.

Francis is the author of numerous articles on interpersonal dynamics, organizational change, and Native Americans. He is currently completing several projects including *Indian Time: Important People and Events Among the American Indians* in conjunction with a book, *Oh Great Spirits: An American Indian's Book of Contemporary Prayers, Chants, and Meditations.*

This Business of Columbus

**by Paula Gunn Allen and Lee Francis III
with the assistance of Mary Allen Francis**

That was All Indian Elementary school I went to, though. . . . They taught White history. I remember later on they had in there Columbus discovered America an' I said, "Why am I saying Columbus discovered America? Hell," I said, "I'm the one discovered America."

—Filbert Anderson, *News from Native California* 5 (Feb./Apr.): 2, 1991.

On the anniversary of five hundred years of Anglo-European progress we invite our fellow citizens to celebrate the arrival of Chris Columbus. This invitation might seem odd, given that we are members of a sovereign American Indian tribe.

Let us consider just what we are celebrating. We are not in fact commemorating the discovery of a hemisphere, since, after all, the Western Hemisphere has been inhabited for well over thirty thousand years. Rather, we are celebrating a unique event: the opening of the "New World" markets. What was going on "over there" in post-feudal Europe during the time Chris was bopping around trying to find a new route to the Far East? Back then, the European nations were in much the same place economically as the good ol' U.S.A. is today. The folks in Europe had depleted most of their natural resources, with no new wealth being created, and their population was increasing at a rate that strained the system of production and distribution to the max. The conventional game plan of the time called for one power group to steal another's wealth.

The great variety of monarchies and religious organizations in Europe at the time required funds to increase their power bases and support their petty quarrels. They needed a vast new source of revenue. The merchants hit on the strategy of finding new products and resources to keep their economy afloat. One of the products they knew would sell like hotcakes was spice.

Bereft of fast-food eateries, the ordinary European cook was stuck with preparing the same old bland tasteless food day after day. These cooks had heard about spices from the Far East that could really spiff up a side of unrefrigerated spoiled beef. Spices also perfumed unwashed courtly bodies draped in clothes that were not so much changed as layered as underlayers became too scruffy.

Unfortunately, traveling the eastern trade routes was a real bummer. Blocking the way between Europe and the Far East of Marco Polo was the savage Middle East where a multitude of factions continually killed one another between bouts of writing brilliant poetry, painting some of the world's greatest paintings, encrusting dishes and cups with wondrous jewels, and inventing abstruse mathematical systems that have yet to be deciphered by Western scientists. The upshot was that the scarcity of the spices that dribbled back through this mayhem to the European markets made them very costly indeed.

Understanding that consumers needed spices at affordable prices, the upstanding politicians—a.k.a. monarchs—knowing where their bread was buttered and wigs were powdered, were somewhat concerned. After consulting with risk management analysts, some of the monarchs wisely decided to take a wait-and-see position.

The diddling continued for some time until a wily young entrepreneur by the name of Cristóbal Colón saw a golden opportunity to earn megabucks by developing a cost-efficient, cheaper way to get those spices—by sea. Shrewdly, he realized that he could thus circumvent known dangers and in all likelihood cut the merchants' costs substantially in the bargain. Preparing a comprehensive business plan backed up by an arcane map from the Middle East that his father had left him, Chris approached several monarchs.

Discouragingly, he was stonewalled by all until he finally got through to the monarchs of Spain and Portugal. Ferdinand was lukewarm on the venture, but Isabella was intrigued. Like many powerful women, she knew a chance for power enhancement when she saw it. After doing lunch with the brash, bold hunk Chris, she decided to provide the venture capital for his enterprise. The capital outlay Isabella decided on barely provided for three tiny ships, some fast-rotting food, and an assortment of hard-laboring prisoners as deck personnel. This last was seen as a benefit because it addressed the problem of prison overcrowding which plagued Isabella.

Triumphant, Trader Chris, the consummate entrepreneur, sounded the clarion call to "go east young man, go west," and promptly set sail. After suffering seasickness, scurvy, rickets, and mutiny, among other trials and travails, good ol' Chris arrived at what is now known as Hispaniola, at the far eastern end of the Caribbean chain (off the coast of Florida). There he met Hatuay, Chief Executive Officer (CEO) of the Island Arawak people.

As CEO, equivalent to a monarch in his own right, Hatuay had no difficulty getting a take on Trader Chris. Hatuay correctly surmised that the great colonizer was intent on initiating a hostile takeover. Chris, operating from what he hoped would become a position of strength, renamed the people he met "Indians," thus strongly implying that their name for themselves was irrelevant. His ploy confirmed Hatuay's hunch that Trader Chris was the forerunner of hordes of mercantilists to come. Chris was a man with a mission: cheap spice.

It didn't take Trader Chris very long to figure out that where he was wasn't where he had hoped to be. Quick on his feet, our main man looked around and saw lumber for buildings, pulp for paper, and wondrously healthy people for cost-effective domestic help, sideshows, and some of the more physically onerous tasks the European serfs were too weak and undernourished to perform. His business sense told him he could really beef up the labor force on the home front for a fraction of the cost of European rates. Chris was certain he could easily market the eye-popping resources he'd stumbled on.

Venture capitalist Isabella was tremendously excited when she heard of Chris's return. Her excitement soon soured when she discovered he didn't bring back the goods. Bummed out because she had been looking forward to eating a slab of lamb without having to endure the rank smell, and dreading the bath she realized she'd have to take, Isabella grew cranky. This was Trader Chris's golden opportunity to close the deal of the centuries.

On his journey back to the good "Old World" Chris had plenty of time to prepare a rousing dog and pony show, and so began schmoozing. He told Isabella and a carefully selected group of potential investors about the forests, the rich soil, the unspoiled pastoral beauty, and the willing, gentle people he had encountered. He even had some representative samples of the latter to display. His rap about the gold in them thar hills clinched the deal.

So, although Chris's presentation skills were somewhat shaky, Isabella and Company decided to ante up some more venture capital and gave Chris a promotion. He was proud to be named a Senior V.I.P. of New World Markets. However, the queen made it clear that Chris had best not come back empty-handed if he wanted to continue enjoying the capacity to breathe in and out. Now a captain of industry and living in the fast lane at last, Chris was determined to bring all the wealth from the New World to his new business investors.

Back in the New World, CEO Hatuay had been conducting a public relations campaign among the Island Arawak people. In repeated public appearances he bad-rapped Colonial Enterprises to his constituents. It was Hatuay's intention to "pink slip" the adventurers Chris had left behind due to a lack of viable transportation facilities when he returned to Spain to promote the American dream with his tales of gold.

Acting on their CEO's signals, the Island Arawak people permanently terminated their association with Chris's displaced personnel. Unfortunately the Arawak public wasn't interested in instituting stringent immigration control policies. This failure to develop a quality immigration program enabled Trader Chris, on his return, to go for the gold.

With Chris busy wheeling and dealing, Colonial Enterprises developed personnel problems. Collective bargaining had not yet evolved, so Chris, following monarchical procedure and setting the example for enterprising capitalists to come, had some of the more difficult personnel hung. Even though he was engaged in island hopping in search of additional products to market in the Old World, Trader Chris also found time to establish the first European slum city in the New World. In a masterful stroke of public relations suck-up, he named the place Isabella.

A scant three centuries after that first eventful takeover, thirteen multinational corporations—known as colonies—were established up shore on the northern mainland in the New World. Originally organized as small business enterprises, these corporations had over the previous century and a half grown rapidly through effective exploitation of easily available natural resources. These enterprises were especially enhanced following extensive hands-on training and skills development workshops in agribusiness conducted by the Powhatans. One of the more successful skills workshops was "The Plantation System: Developing Tobacco Crops for Export."

By 1776, the thirteen developing multinational corporations split off from their Old World parent companies and went public. To raise sufficient capital for their endeavors, they hit on a dynamic marketing campaign. Products such as timber, sassafras, pharmaceuticals, chocolate, corn, tomatoes, potatoes, and other new foods, and new technologies were exported to the eager consumers of the Old World. This burgeoning enterprise gave the fledgling corporations an over 50-percent share in the world market for food and pharmaceuticals alone. Just think, without the efforts of that daring entrepreneur Christopher Columbus, the blessings of progress and prosperity might never have come to the Old World.

Fast forward and notice the many parallels between today's post-industrial U.S. of A. and those struggling economies of the Europe of yesteryear. Like them, we have depended on and without remorse exploited what were, five hundred years ago, unlimited natural resources to fuel our economy, our government, and our way of life. Like Europe of five hundred years ago, the remaining natural resources are dangerously depleted and so our entrepreneurs of today are forced to zealously build paper empires through mergers, acquisitions, junk bond buy-outs, and arms and drug sales instead of creating new products.

The natural resources that once seemed unlimited are rapidly dwindling. The magnificent forests are gone. The grasslands have become shopping centers and planned communities. The buffalo appears only on the nickel. The gold has been ripped from the earth and buried at Fort Knox. The bald eagle and the spotted owl are endangered species. The air is poisoned. The land is poisoned. The sea is poisoned. The ozone layer is thinning and all of life is drowning in a sea of pollution.

The flourishing population of original inhabitants of North America was decimated by diseases such as venereal disease, smallpox, and tuberculous— all gifts of the civilized Old World. Hundreds of thousands of the native people were kidnapped, enslaved, raped, murdered, or massacred by the noble civilized folks from the Old World. They died by the thousands as they were forcibly marched to concentration camps (euphemistically known as reservations, forts, agencies, and boarding schools). Those who survived the marches died from starvation by the thousands during the early years of reservation life. Today, many of the survivors continue to die of diabetes, tuberculosis, alcoholism, and drugs. The Western Old World's policy of internal apartheid and genocide ensured a guaranteed profit margin for mercantile interests.

It is impossible to engage in extensive land development projects without encountering native outcries. The issues of tribal sovereignty, violation of fishing, hunting, and water treaty rights and of land ownership are largely ignored by media and progressives alike. The Old World's aggressive disinformation campaign conducted over five hundred years has effectively eliminated awareness of true American history. A recent debate concerning the relative value of a golf course versus the sacredness of Indian burial grounds is the latest example of the forces militating against protection of the biosphere and against the deeply human values of respect for the dead, the land, and the life of the spirit. Only through the continued destruction of the planet can the Anglo-European Old World fulfill its manifest destiny and keep out of the red.

All of this we owe to trader supreme and entrepreneur par excellence, Christopher Columbus, Cristóbal Colón, who was the first representative of the mercantile interests of the Old World to the New World. Now, both the Old and New Worlds have become one exploited and abused world.

A major way for Americans to celebrate the anniversary of the Senior V.I.P. of New World Markets' contact with the New World is to recognize that the true bottom line is not ever-expanding markets. Rather, we must engage in serious, organized efforts to clean up the mess mercantilism has created, return to the planet-centered social systems and the world view of the tribal peoples, and denounce for all time America's internal apartheid system.

Christopher Columbus died in prison, broke, syphilitic, alone. He enjoyed his celebrity all too briefly. His queen tired of her brave new man, and turned to more noble compatriots to expand her position. The fate of Chris, the man who became the prototype and hero of New World expansion, is the fate that mercantile nations will ultimately face if the lesson of Chris's life is not heeded.

Instead of progress, let us celebrate freedom, the critically important freedom of all beings to live in harmonious balance so that all people may live.

Ah-ho.